Amazon Echo Guide
The Ultimate Amazon Echo User Guide for Your Smart Home with Alexa (2017 updated user guide, Echo Manual, with latest updates, web services, user manual)

JOHN EDWARDS

CONTENTS

Introduction

The greatest feature of the Amazon Echo is that you can customize it to your daily routine and lifestyle. It is an amazing smart device that gives you a lot of possibilities to make your life more convenient, smart, fun and easy.

Alexa is designed to be a full integration between the developer and device. It enables to explore the voice-driven behaviors via the Alexa Skill Kit. The main goal of Amazon's approach is to let the developers add new Skills for Alexa and learn how to integrate them.

Alexa has a wide range of functionality. It may be programmed for such customer service situations like ticketing, banking, parking, and purchasing food products at a large grocery store. Alexa is easy for interaction as you can ask her questions and it can perform lots of commands. Alexa may be also incorporated by the banks into an Automatic Teller to enable customers to ask a range of questions about their balances or transactions.

The Amazon Echo Dot is simple and sleek. It is a truly innovative device that is able to make your world fun and smart.

Having Alexa at its core, the Amazon Echo is getting better and better. This Alexa enabled device can be customized with the skills that respond your lifestyle most of all. Your Echo will enable you to be productive and get things done. You can check schedules, update events, order supplies and much more with Amazon Echo.

In this guide you will learn many things about Alexa, including how Echo can integrate with your smart home devices. In simple guide we will teach you all the basics to make your home smart and how to create smart skills. After reading this guide, you will know that the Echo is more than just a speaker.

In this guide you will also know about the difference between the Amazon Echo and the Google Home. You will learn about their advantages and disadvantages.

You will learn how many things you can do with your Echo. You can not only listen to music with the Amazon Echo and ask various questions, you can also book tickets, order items from Amazon, check the traffic state, weather forecast, order pizza, Uber, control the lights in your home and many other helpful things that make your life smart, fun and convenient.

Chapter 1: The Basics of Setting Up Your Amazon Echo

The Amazon Echo is designed for a simple and seamless set up.

Before installing your Echo at home, you should first download the Alexa App. You can download it free from the appropriate app stores or from http://alexa.amazon.com for desktop users. You can change a variety of settings with the Alexa App and you can also communicate with Alexa.

After downloading the Alexa App, you should install Echo into your home. First, you should find a suitable location that meets some requirements: it must be at least 8 inches (20cm) from any walls, windows or other electronic devices that could cause interference (e.g. your microwave).

Once it's done, plug the adapter in and connect to the power outlet. The Echo's light ring will become blue before turning orange and then Alexa will greet you.

Then you should connect to Wi-Fi. Echo is not able to connect to mobile hotspots or Ad-hoc (peer to peer) networks. You should follow these steps to connect your Echo with a Wi-Fi network.

1) First, open the Alexa App, then open the left-hand-side navigation panel and choose *Settings* from the options. Select your device and choose *Set up a new device.*

2) Then press on your Echo device and hold the *Action* button for 5 seconds. The Light Ring will change to orange whilst your device connects.

3) Then return to the Alexa App. You will see the list of Wi-Fi networks available for you to connect. If you cannot see your Network, you should choose *Rescan* or *Add a Network* from the bottom of the list.

You should also choose your wake word before you start using the Amazon Echo. When you call Alexa she knows you need something. According to the default settings the Echo responds to Alexa but you can change to either Echo or Alexa. To enable it you should follow these steps:

1) First, open the Alexa App and open the left-hand-side navigation panel. Then select *Settings* and choose your device. Then scroll through the options and select *Wake Word*. You should choose your desired wake word from the drop down menu, select Save. And the light ring will flash orange.

<u>The Light Ring</u>

The Echo has a light ring on its top for visual communication with you. Changing its color, Echo is able to display Alexa's status. Here is the table for some of Echo's light ring codes.

Light Arrangement Visible	What it means
All lights off	Amazon Echo is active and ready for requests
Solid blue with spinning cyan	Amazon Echo is starting up

lights	
Solid red light	The microphones are off. (Press the microphone button to turn on the microphones.)
Continuous oscillating violet light	An error occurred during Wi-Fi setup.
Orange light spinning clockwise	Echo is connecting to your Wi-Fi network
Solid blue with cyan pointing in direction of person speaking	Echo is processing your request
White light	You are adjusting the volume level.

What is Power LED

The Power Led is also situated at the top of Echo. It visually shows the Echo's Wi-Fi connection. If you see a solid white light it means that your device has a Wi-Fi connection. If your device has a solid orange light it means there is no Wi-Fi connection. If the Echo has a blinking orange light it means that it is connected to Wi-Fi but it cannot access Alexa.

Microphone off Button

The microphone off button is located at the top of the Echo. If you press it you can turn off the Echo's seven microphones. After this action the light ring turns red.

Action Button

The action button that wakes Alexa is located on the top of the Echo. You can also use it to turn off a timer, your alarm and put it into Wi-Fi mode if you hold it for five seconds.

Volume Ring

To increase Alexa's volume you should turn the volume ring clockwise and turn counter-clockwise to decrease the volume. The light ring usually displays the volume level.

Bluetooth Settings

The Echo has Bluetooth compatibility so you can connect it to your mobile device simply by saying *"Pair"*. Before requesting Alexa to pair, make sure that the Bluetooth on your mobile device is activated. If you desire to disconnect, simply use the command: *"Disconnect"*.

How to Use Multiple Devices Right

You should know that there is no need to connect Alexa enabled devices as they run the same. But you can enable up to 12 different Alexa-enabled devices, using the Alexa app, as each device is registered to your Amazon account. Follow these recommendations to use multiple Alexa-enabled devices right.

You should choose different wake words for the devices, for example, your Echo and Echo Dot that are installed within speaking range of each other. If they have the same wake word you should make sure that they are located at least 30 feet apart. Then you should use the Alexa app or the Voice Remote for Amazon Echo to request one specific device.

If you have Fire TV devices and Amazon Tap you should give each device a distinct name to prevent any confusion.

You should be aware of the content sharing across Alexa devices. It is being improved by Amazon at this moment. But for this moment all the content shared between devices may be seen on the Alexa App in the settings menu. You cannot also customize which content is available to some device. Here is the list of the content that may be share across your Amazon account:

- ➤ Flash briefing
- ➤ Music and media
- ➤ Shopping
- ➤ Smart Home Devices
- ➤ To Do Lists
- ➤ Household profiles

And here is the content that may not be shared across your Amazon account:

- ➤ Alarms
- ➤ Wake Words
- ➤ Sounds
- ➤ Bluetooth connections

Software Updates

To keep your Alexa updated you should continuously look for the new software. Before downloading you have to check which version you have installed. Follow these steps:

First, open Alexa App and then open the left hand side navigation panel. Then you should choose *Settings* and select your device. Then scroll down until *Device Software Version* is shown.

Before downloading the most recent software updates you

should make sure that your Echo is switched on and has an active Wi-Fi connection. You must avoid giving commands to your device while installing the new software.

When the update is ready to be installed the light ring will turn blue. The time of the software installation may vary and it depends on the speed of your Wi-Fi connection.

Chapter 2: The Amazon Echo's Capabilities

How to Get Flight and Transportation Information with your Echo

If you are planning your trip the Echo is also able to help you with it. For example, you can obtain flight information. You don't need to pick up your mobile device as Alexa is able to look for the flights. You just need to use your voice and tell the information about the flight that would suit you best, depending on the upcoming trip information and the options for pricing.

You can set your home airport within Alexa to make sure that your flight information is accurate and personal.

Here are the skills that work in conjunction with Alexa to help you in travel and to provide you with flight information:

1. **Landing Times:** You can get landing times free once you have enabled it. And you can get flight information based on flight numbers. Here is the list of the airlines that it supports: Virgin America, Spirit, United, Frontier, Alaska, Delta, Air Canada, American, Southwest, Hawaiian and Porter.

   You can simply say: *"Alexa, ask Landing Times when Southwest flight ...(number of flight) lands"*

   Skyscanner: If you enable Skyscanner you can get estimated pricing before beginning the actual booking process as this flight search skill is free to enable. It usually shows the most recent lowest prices found.

   You can say: *"Alexa, ask Skyscanner to find me a flight to Los Angeles tomorrow"*

2. **Kayak**: You can get the real time flight information with the use of Kayak's flight tracker. You can also check the prices of rental cars and hotels along with flight information

   You can ask: *"Alexa, where can I go for $400?"*

3. **Flight Guru**: Flight Guru gives flight information based on flight number. When you use the flight number you can get the flight status and landing information.

Setting Up Your Alexa to Receive Flight Information w/ Kayak

1. First, open the Alexa mobile application from your mobile device or tablet.
2. Then select Skills from the left menu.
3. Search for 'Kayak' and select the newly found skill.
4. Then select 'Enable Skill' from the Skill's home screen.
5. After enabling this skill in the application you can use with your Alexa enabled Echo.
6. Once you have enabled this skill you will be able to search and get pricing using the regular Alexa voice commands.

Here is the list of commands for this skill in statements or questions:

- "Alexa, ask Kayak where I can go for $250"
- "Alexa, ask Kayak when the Flight from New York will land in London"
- "Alexa, ask Kayak how much it cost to fly from Los Angeles to Toronto"

Setting Up Your Alexa to Receive Flight Information w/ Sky Scanner

1. First, open the Alexa mobile application from your mobile device or tablet.
2. Then select Skills from the left menu.
3. Find 'SkyScanner' and select the newly found skill.
4. Then you should select 'Enable Skill' from the Skill's home screen.
5. Once you have enabled the skill in the application you can use it with your Alexa enabled Echo.
6. After enabling this skill, you can search and get pricing using the regular Alexa voice commands.

Here are the commands for this skill may include statements or questions:

- "Alexa, ask Sky Scanner to find me a flight for Friday to New York"
- "Alexa, ask SkyScanner where I can go this Monday"
- "Alexa, open SkyScanner"

You should know that these skills will not take you through the booking process as they are only for informational purposes.

How to Use Your Amazon Echo to Read with Kindle

If you are a keen reader the Echo may become a good companion to add some books to any library or study. You can use Echo to read an eligible selection of books with its text-to-speech technology, many other news articles and Wikipedia articles.

Here is the list of eligible selections that you can read using the Amazon Echo:

- Items from the Kindle Owners' Lending Library
- Items shared I your Family Library
- Items borrowed through Kindle Unlimited
- Items purchased from the Kindle Store

You can also find eligible Alexa Books in the Alexa mobile application. You can do it by selecting Music & Books > Kindle Books > Books Alexa can read.

For this moment, reading of comic books, speed of narration control and immersion reading are not supported by Alexa.

When you tell Alexa to read books you should know that Alexa will not start the book over again. She will read from the point at which you left off in any Amazon Devices.

You can also move to different chapter in the book by utilizing the Now Playing bar that may be done within Alexa application. And you can also choose a chapter from the queue list.

Here is the number of commands that you can tell Alexa to interact with Kindle through the Amazon Echo:

- "Read my book, [insert book title here]"
- "Play the Kindle book, [insert book title]"

- "Read [insert book title]"
- "Go back" – if you want to go to a previous paragraph
- "Go forward" – it means to go to the next paragraph
- "Play"
- "Skip back" – it means to go to a previous paragraph
- "Skip ahead" – it means to go to the next paragraph
- "Stop"
- "Pause"
- "Next" – it means to go to the next paragraph
- "Previous" – it means to go to a previous paragraph

Setting up You Amazon Echo with Kindle

1. You should open the Kindle Application from your mobile device in order to start this process.
2. Then you should select **Music & Books** from the left navigation menu.
3. Then select Kindle Books from the bottom of the menu.
4. You can see only the supported Kindle Books under the heading, Books Alexa Can Read.
5. Then you should Select one of the supported books from the list and Alexa will start to read on the Echo Dot.

How to Use Your Echo for References

If you need to know the definition of any word or you are not sure about spelling of some word the Amazon Echo is able to help you with it. It can perform a great variety of skills that may help you with spelling words, getting facts, defining words and many other skills.

Even without enabling any of these skills the Echo can give you answers to dictionary and spelling related questions. Here is the list of command that may help you to search information you need:

"Alexa, spell the word "miscellaneous"

"Alexa, what is the definition of the word "miscellaneous"?"

And here are the skills that provide this functionality:

1. **Word of the Day:** You can enable this skill free and get a word everyday with definitions and examples

from the website wordnik.com. If you want to use this skill with Alexa , just say:

    a. "Alexa, ask Word of the Day for today's word"

    b. "Alexa, open Word of the Day"

2. **Quick Word Spell**: Once you have enabled this skill free you can get the spelling of words on the fly and as needed. You should just say the following commands to use this skill:

    a. "Alexa, ask Quick Word to spell "squirrel""

    b. "Alexa, ask Quick Word to spell "crocodile""

3. **Word Source**: You can get to know about the origin of words with this skill. If you need to use this skill you should simply say:

    a. "Alexa, ask Word Source about the word basket"

    b. "Alexa, ask Word Source what is the origin of the "chassis""

How to Group Your Smart Home Devices

One of the advantages of the Amazon Echo is that you can use it with your smart home devices. After grouping your devices together you can easily control multiple devices and multiple rooms at once.

You can to create a group of smart home devices within the Alexa application to be able to control multiple smart home devices all at once.

How to create a Smart Home Group on Your Echo

1. You should open the Alexa mobile application from your mobile device and locate Smart Home from your left navigation panel in the Alexa app.
2. Then select the term Groups from the menu > Create Groups.
3. Then you should enter your anticipated group name. You usually use the room names to give your group a recognizable name. If you need to group every smart item connected in the bedroom you should name your group mastered.

4. Once you have named the group you can select the devices in which you would like to add to this group. You should select Add once you have completed.

Once you have created your group in the Alexa app you can use commands via Alexa with it. If you need to use some skill you should say to Alexa "Open [skill name]" before she recognizes your request and complete it. Here is the list of sample commands you can use with your smart home devices:

"Set [Group Name] to [#]%"
"Turn on [Smart Device Name or group]"

You can manage your device scene through the desired device's companion application. You can see the scene names in the Smart Home section of the Alexa app. You can also edit Smart Groups within the Alexa Application. You can do it easily by under Groups by selecting the group you would like to edit. If you want to make changes to the name you should select the desired group and edit the text information. In case if you need to change the items within the group you should select or deselect the checkbox next to the application. And if you need to delete the grouping you should select Delete.

How to Use Your Echo Dot with Wikipedia

Wikipedia is one of the most reliable and popular resources that widespread all over the world. It gets over 500 million

monthly views every day and its information is edited and updated by the users all the time. If you like to know something new from Wikipedia the Amazon Echo can also work with it without using any skill. It is simple to use the Echo in conjunction with Wikipedia. And if you want your Echo to read a passage from Wikipedia you should say: "Alexa – Wikipedia [topic]". This command is meant to search the topic.

The Echo will read a passage to the requested topic. But Alexa will not read the whole article, only a short passage. If you want Alexa to continue reading this article, you say "More" or "hear more".

You can also get information another way from Alexa and Wikipedia by saying: "Alexa, Wikipedia [Name of the Article]". And Alexa will read the article you need.

How to Use Your Echo for Radio Programs

As you know the Amazon Echo works with different media applications and you can also utilize the for listening to local radio stations.

You can listen to live radio streams through the Echo without any account sign up or setup, using the integration with TuneIn. If you like listening to the radio then you should create a free TuneIn Account. Having your new account, you can follow your favorite stations. They will be available when your Echo is performing a search and moves them to the top of the results.

The Echo is able to recognize and to find live radio stations even if the podcasts are limited to the items featured on TuneIn. If you want to begin listening to a radio station using Alexa, you should say, "Alexa, play [number on the dial] [station name]".

Besides, the Echo may be used as an internet radio. Using a simple command, you can enable the radio to play within seconds. TuneIn is a defaults database for streaming radio. If you ask Alexa to play some station it will repeat the station you asked for to make sure you it is correct. Alexa may also ask for confirmation.

You should know that your Echo does not come with a tuner and all radio programs are streamed via your Wi-Fi connection. The weak signal may hinder your ability to clearly listen to programs. But if your connection speeds are good, you can have good signal. You can use your Echo as a bedside radio and attach headphones at leisure.

How to Use TuneIn

If you want to start listening to the radio or podcasts via your Amazon Echo you do not need a TuneIn account as your Echo is able to do it without it. The TuneIn Library is large enough to meet any expectations and tastes. It is ready for your exploration. You should know the name of the podcast you would like to listen to and the Echo is ready to play it. Here are some sample commands that you can tell to get the most out of TuneIn, using your Echo:

"Alexa, play [Podcast Name] podcast on TuneIn."

"Alexa, play the podcast [insert podcast name here]."

These commands work great if you know the name of the show you are searching for.

There are also two ways you can use to search for podcasts via TuneIn. You can do it within the Alexa application or via the TuneIn Website. When you have found something you are interested in, you should use the commands above to start listening on your Echo or its connected Bluetooth Speaker.

Listening to a particular podcast is easier than listening to the podcasts in a specific order. You can use the Alexa App as a remote to control which podcast should play first, second, etc. After listening to the backlog of podcasts you may be offered a show. Then you can return to using Alexa to play the newest episodes.

How to Use IHeartRadio

You can choose lots of music that you would like to listen to, access a variety of live radio stations and create your very own radio station, using this application.

IHeartRadio is able to play your favorite jams without stopping. Once you have given your station options it will find similar music to play on your station. This list of available songs includes over 20 million tracks.

It is easy to create an IHeartRadio account. You can also use your Facebook or Gmail accounts for quick creation. Once you have completed with your account you should simply link within the Alexa App to utilize with your Amazon Echo.

Here are the sample commands:

"Alexa, play Fox Sports Radio on iHeartRadio."

"Alexa, open IHeartRadio"

How to Use Pandora Radio

Pandora is another radio streaming service which is able to serve as the Echo's default music source unlike Spotify. When you give the command to Alexa she must specify which streaming service to choose to play your request from. And if the service is left out she will use the default option. If you have not updated the default Alexa will try to play the item from Amazon Music. You should navigate to the Music section of the Alexa mobile application to update your default application. You should open your settings and select 'Music & Media'. Then you should choose the button which reads "Choose Default Music Services" within this section. If you have not subscribed to Amazon Prime you need to do it to ensure your music is coming from the right application.

You should follow these to set up Pandora or your Amazon Echo:

1. First you should navigate to the Alexa app.
2. Then select the Menu button. You can see the button in the left corner of the application. Then select Music & Books and select Pandora.
3. Then, from the registration page, you should select the "Link your account now" Button
   1. If you have not created your account you should select "Create a Pandora Account". Then fill out the needed information to complete the registration process.
   2. If you have an account simply you should select "I have a Pandora Account". Then you should enter in your associated Pandora email address and password. Then proceed by tapping "Look Up Account".

Once you have completed this process, you will see that your current station list will appear within the Alexa Application. If you want to utilize Pandora with the Amazon Echo, you should use some commands below:

"Alexa, I like this song"

"Alexa, thumbs down this song"

"Alexa, play [Artist Name] radio on Pandora"

You should also know that usual items like Stop, Pause, resume work the same like with normal music play on Alexa.

Chapter 3: Playing Games with your Echo

The Amazon Echo can be used not only for asking information but also for playing games. There are lots of games that you can play with your Echo. Using the Alexa skills portion of the application, you can enable these games. Once you have enabled the game you would need just to say the keywords to start.

Here is the list of games:

Truth or Dare: You can play a classic game of Truth or Die with the help of Alexa. The concept of this game is when a group of people take turns asking each other "Truth or Dare?" To enable this game, just say:

"Alexa, open truth or dare"

"Alexa play truth or dare"

Bingo: You can also play Bingo but you will need bingo cards that you can download from lovemyecho.com in PDF format. When your Echo call out the bingo numbers for the entire game you should simply respond with "Next" to keep the game continue.

When you want to start playing this game you should say "Alexa, open Bingo". When you want to continue the game, just say "call the next number".

Tic Tac Toe: You can play Tic Tac Toe on your Echo Dot. It is very easy as you can remember your positioning. You should to sketch the moves while you are playing. You can recorder the moves using the following positioning:

Top Left | Top | Top Right

Left | Center | Right

Bottom Left | Bottom | Bottom Right

When you are ready to start a game with Alexa, just say "Alexa, let's play tic tac toe"

Blackjack: You can play numerous rounds of blackjack while Alexa keeps track of your bankroll. There are different versions of blackjack. For example, blackjack by Garrett Vargas starts with 5000 credits and adds and subtracts during the game.

If you don't know the rules Alexa can read them and give the basic game strategy. You can enable the game of blackjack by saying such command:

"Alexa, start a game of black jack"

Jeopardy: You can freely enable this skill as it is easy to add it from the skills section within the Alexa application to the Echo. You can start game by saying, "Alexa, start Jeopardy".

This game includes lots of questions from different categories. The categories may be sports, history, travel and even pop culture. And the answers should be in the question form.

Chapter 4: Getting Various Information

If you want to know some general information you even don't need to setup any of the skills. Alexa can perform a lot of general commands. Here are the basic commands:

"Alexa, stop.": If you want Alexa to stop activity it is performing or to close out music that is playing you should say this command. It concerns such activities as playing music, playing some game or generally performing some skill.

"Alexa, turn volume to 10"/ "Alexa, volume seven.": This command enables to turn the volume up or down between zero and ten without touching the volume button.

You can also say such commands like "Alexa, turn it up" or "Alexa turn it down" to control the sound.

"Alexa, please mute."/ "Alexa, please unmute.": If you need to mute and unmute the volume on the device, simple say this command.

"Alexa, cancel.": You can cancel any activity that Alexa is going to perform with this command. You can also say "stop" instead of "cancel".

"Alexa, what's my Flash Brief?": You can get news according to the settings you have made with your flash briefings in the Alexa mobile application.

"Alexa, what's headlining in the news?": You can get information about what is currently headlining in the news.

"Alexa, what's the weather for today?": You can ask about weather forecast for today or tomorrow or ask the probability of rain today by saying: "Alexa, what is the chance that it will rain today?" or "Alexa, do I need an umbrella this week?"

If you need a weather forecast for upcoming weekend you can ask: "Alexa, what's the weather for this upcoming weekend?"

While cooking or when you need it, you can ask Alexa basic measurement questions even without setting any skills.

Here are the measurement questions you can ask:

"How many tea spoons in one soup-spoon?"

"Alexa, how many cups in a pint?"

"How many miles are from New York to Chicago?"

Alexa has got vast knowledge in many spheres. You can ask any kind of questions and get to know the scores of latest matches in basketball, baseball and other sport related question.

Without involving any skills, Alexa is ready to answer all your questions and she can also do minor conversions and simple math.

Easter Eggs

You should know that not all features within the Echo or within Alexa are spelled out in nice detailed lists. There are things which are still left to be discovered. Easter eggs are weird phrases and jokes that Alexa will respond to. The new Easter eggs are added every day.

Here is the list of Easter Eggs that you can use with Alexa. These phrases are taken from Reddit and compiled by users of the site.

1. "Alexa, do you know Glados?"
2. "Alexa, what is the meaning of life?"
3. "Alexa, who lives in a pineapple under the sea?"
4. "Alexa, is there a Santa?"
5. "Alexa, do aliens exist?"
6. "Alexa, where do you live?"
7. "Alexa, what is love?"
8. "Alexa, what is your quest?"
9. "Alexa, do you know Hal?"
10. "Alexa, what is your favorite color?"
11. "Alexa, which comes first: the chicken or the egg?"
12. "Alexa, can you give me some money?"
13. "Alexa, do you want to fight?"
14. "Alexa, do you know the muffin man?"
15. "Alexa, where are you from?"
16. "Alexa, how much do you weigh?"
17. "Alexa, why did the chicken cross the road?"
18. "Alexa, where are my keys?"
19. "Alexa, who let the dogs out?"
20. "Alexa, how tall are you?"
21. "Alexa, why do birds suddenly appear?"
22.. "Alexa, will you be my girlfriend?"

23. "Alexa, who's the boss?"

24. "Alexa, is there life on Mars?"

25. "Alexa, do you want to go on a date?"

26. "Alexa, what are you wearing?"

27. "Alexa, give me a hug."

28. "Alexa, what is the sound of one hand clapping?"

29. "Alexa, what are you made of?"

30. "Alexa, what should I wear today?"

You can find more Easter Eggs on Amazon website or other websites.

Asking about Weather & Other General Information

 Whenever you have a busy morning when you are in a hurry for work and you don't have enough time to check some things, Alexa is ready to help you with it. She can provide you with the latest information about weather so you could know what to wear and to remind you to check your phone or tell you the time. You don't need to touch your phone as Alexa can tell you all this information.

You can use the following command to get to know all necessary general information:

- *"Alexa, what's the weather in New York?" or "Alexa what's the weather?"* Alexa is able to provide you with the weather information for your current address area if you haven't a specified the city. If you have specified the city, she can give the forecast for that area.

- *Alexa, what's the time?* Alexa can tell you the current time without any extra details.

- *Alexa, what is my commute?* You can use this command if you have set your home and work address within the Alexa application. If you ask this Alexa is able to provide you with the current traffic and route information along with an estimated time.

Chapter 5: All about Alexa Skills

The Echo can utilize a great number of Amazon Skills to prove it is truly smart home device. These skills include different categories:

- Food & Drink
- Games & Trivia
- Health & Fitness
- Lifestyle
- Local
- Movies & TV
- Music & Audio
- News

- Humor
- Productivity
- Shopping
- Smart Home
- Social
- Sports
- Travel & Transportation
- Utilities
- Weather
- Business & Finance
- Communication
- Education & Reference

Food & Drink

The Amazon Echo has many skills to use for food and drink. They include items that provide current drink specials, recipes or even the means to order food. The ordering of pizza and even wings is still one of the most popular features in the food section.

Wingstop:

If you enable the Wingstop skill you will be able to order wings a cinch. You can order wings from recent orders or from your set favorites.

But first you must have a linked Wingstop account to use this skill. Using this account, you can manage your favorite orders as well as any payment information needed to make orders.

Alexa is able to guide you through the entire order process. Once you have placed your order Alexa will also provide information when your order will be available and send a confirmation email. You can enable this skill by simply saying the following commands:

"Alexa, ask Wingstop to order 4-piece spicy wing combo"

"Alexa, ask Wingstop to order my favorite"

Pizza Hut:

Using the Pizza Hut skill, you can have a pizza at your door within the hour without picking up a phone. First, you must have a linked Pizza Hut account to be able to use this skill. You can manage your favorite orders as well as any payment information needed to make orders with the help of your account. You can also order from the menu.

Before ordering from Pizza Hut you should make sure that you have a delivery address and a default payment method on your pizza hut account.

Here are simple commands to order pizza:

"Alexa, open Pizza Hut"

"Alexa, ask Pizza Hut to reorder my last order"

Domino's Pizza:

This is one of the most advertised and popular Alexa skills. You can not only place the most recent order but also to check the status of your order using the Domino's Tracker that is currently available only in the United States.

You also need an account with Dominoes to continue with order placement, like with previous skills. You should link this account in the Alexa application as well. If you want to place an order through Alexa you must have a recent order or have an Easy Order saved. You should enter all of your pertinent information like your address, credit card and phone number into your pizza profile on the Domino's website.

You will need your phone number to track your order and receive the status. It is easy to enable this application for ordering by simply saying:

"Alexa, open Domino's"
"Alexa, open Domino's and place my most recent order"

Business & Finance

Any user can find something helpful among business and finance skills of the Echo, depending on his lifestyle and needs. The Echo is able to perform such skill when the user can get the updated economical and insurance information. Here are some sample applications:

Capital One: You can ask about your credit card, bank account, home or auto loans using the Capital One. Using this skill, you can also easily know where you are spending the most money. The Capital One includes many commands. But you must first log into Capital One from within the Alexa application to create the linkage if you want to start using this skill.

When you want to ask about your Credit Card you should use the following Alexa commands:

"Alexa, how much did I spend at [insert store name] last week?"

"Alexa, how much did I spend last month at [insert store name]?"

"Alexa, ask Capital One what is my credit card balance."

"Alexa, ask Capital One when is my credit card bill due?"

When you want to ask about your banking account, use the following Alexa commands:

"Alexa, ask Capital One, what are my recent transactions?"

"Alexa, ask Capital One, what is my checking account balance?"

When you want to ask about your automotive loan, use the following Alexa commands:

"Alexa ask Capital One, what is my payoff quote?"

"Alexa ask Capital One, when is my car loan due?"

"Alexa ask Capital One, what is my s my car loan principal?"

When you want to ask about your home loan, use the following Alexa commands:

"Alexa, ask Capital One, when is my next mortgage payment due?"

"Alexa, ask Capital One, what is the principal on my mortgage?"

Nationwide Insurance: If you want to know the information about auto insurance products and contact information for quotes the Nationwide Alexa skill will help you with it. Here are some common statements to enable Nationwide:

"Alexa, open Nationwide"

"Tell me about primary coverages"

Real Estate

If you need to find home, to buy or rent within a specific area this application will provide you this information. To enable this application you should first create an account and sign up with Voiceter Pro. Once you have created the account and linked with Alexa you can search for homes but receive contact information from local realtors. Here are some common statements to enable Real Estate:

"Alexa, open Real Estate"

"Alexa, tell Real Estate to buy some house in Los Angeles"

Communication

Using the communication section of the skills houses items you can send messages, receive notifications and provide facts.

Here are the items that some of these skills include: A T&T messages, Programming facts, Hindi tutor and secret keeper.

AT&T Send Message:

You can use this application with a Post Paid AT&T mobile phone. But first you must connect your AT&T wireless account to provide proper work for this skill. You can add 10 frequent contacts as message recipients. Here are some common statements to enable AT&T Send Message:

"Alexa, open AT&T"

"Alexa, ask AT&T to text my mother"

"Alexa, ask AT&T to text my son"

Message Wall:

This application enables the users of Echo products to send anonymous message to one and another. This skill may not be appropriate for children and they should be monitored closely by parents if the children try to utilize it. Here are some common statements to enable Message Wall:

"Alexa, open Message Wall"
"Alexa, what was the last message on Message Wall"

Education & Reference

This section of the Alexa skills section provides learning and fact type skills. These skills are: quotes, word spells, presidents and various other types. Here are some sample applications:

Computer Geek:

You can know various interesting computer facts with this skill. This application is meant to provide interesting and useful information to the user. You can enable this application free and utilize it easily. Here are some common commands to enable this application include:

"Alexa, ask Computer Geek to tell me something"
"Alexa, ask Computer Geek to give me a fact"

Read the Old Testament This Year:

Using this application, you can read the King James Version of the bible on a regular basis. This skill is designed to start on January 1 and continue throughout the year, reading a scheduled passage each day. Here are some common ways to enable this application:

"Alexa, read the Old Testament"
"Alexa, ask the Old Testament for today's reading"
"Alexa, ask Old Testament to read for November 15"

This Day in History:

This application is brought to Alexa by A&E Television Network. Using this skill, you can know random facts on things that have happen on your current date in history. You can launch this skill by saying the following commands:
"Alexa, launch This Day in History"
"Tell me about another event from August 10"

Travel & Transportation

Uber: The application Uber is designed to make it easy for a user to call for a ride any time. In order to be able to use Uber you must enable it through Alexa in a very specific way.

First, you must create or sign into your existing Uber Account before using Uber via Alexa. Once you have completed it you can use Alexa to change your default pickup location, ask for ride status or cancel an already requested ride. You can also request rides from different Uber accounts.

To enable Uber on your device you should say things like:

"Alexa, ask Uber to change my default pickup location"

"Alexa, ask Uber to request a ride"

"Alexa, ask Uber to call me an Uber SUV from work"

Music

You will also have access the Amazon music library associated with your Amazon account. If you have subscribed to Amazon Prime music, you will be available to use it as well.

You can use the free option TuneIn radio with your Echo Dot. You can connect it with Spotify after subscription. Besides, you can update your default music subscription to be Spotify within the Alexa application.

Chapter 6: How to Use Your Echo with Multiple Devices

It is recommended to use the Echo in conjunction with other devices. It is easy to add a new Echo to the home. You can do it the same way as the initial set up of your first device. When it's time to set up the second device you should log into the Alexa application and navigate to your settings and follow general setup instructions. It is not necessary to go through the set up process again with your second device as the new device will take on the skills of your connected device.

It is also important to place your multiple devices right to get the perfect balance in your home. It may lead to confusion if you place one device in the middle of two standing devices. Controlling all Alexa enabled devices is easy with your voice or through the Alexa app. They are able to respond even if they have the same wake word due to ESP (Echo Spatial Perception). Some versions of the Alexa products do not require a wake word. They are Amazon Tap, Fire tablets, and Fire TV devices.

When interacting with your Echo you can use the Alexa Voice Remote that it sold separately. There is also an option to change your wake word for different devices.

But you should know that not all applications are able to work in sync. All the Alexa enabled devices cannot play music at the same time for full affect. If you have Spotify as your default music source then your devices cannot play the same songs.

You also cannot sync timers and alarms between multiple devices. You should know that every Echo performs independently of one another even the skills are the same between the devices. Bluetooth connections are also set separately.

Not all the function may be synced between Alexa products. But within the Alexa mobile application all the information listed under the Account section is the same for all linked devices. This information includes such options:

- Music & Media Information – It includes information from Amazon Music, Spotify, Pandora, iHeartRadio and TuneIn.
- Flash Briefings – You can get the information for where to get flash briefings from and what areas are turned on.
- Sports Update – You can get information about the teams you would like to know about.
- Traffic – It includes the home information set by the user to provide the route traffic information.
- Shopping and To-do lists
- Calendar

Chapter 7: How to Create Your Smart Home with Alexa

One of the best features of the Amazon Echo is its ability to control smart appliances within the household, such as lights, switches, heaters, and many more. You can group all smart devices for easy and efficient management. After grouping all smart lights in a single group, for example, in the kitchen, you need to say the group name in your voice command. You don't need to separate each device into multiple commands.

The list of compatible smart products is increasing. This

chapter will tell you only about the most common products that are used with the Amazon Echo. As for the other smart technologies, they require "Skills".

Philips Hue

One of the smart products under the Philips brand are Hue bulbs. It is great that they may be controlled and the light colors may be changed too. You can link these devices to the Echo speaker and control the Philips Hue bulbs through voice commands.

Before starting controlling them you should make sure that they are connected to the same Wi-Fi network. You should go to the Alexa app and search for the bulbs. You can use the Philips user guide to know how to connect the Philips Hue to your Wi-Fi network.

After pairing the bulbs with the Echo, you can use the following commands to control the lights:

Alexa, turn off the lights.
Alexa, dim the lights to 50 percent.

After grouping the lights you can use the following variant for your voice command:

Alexa, switch on [group name].

SmartThings

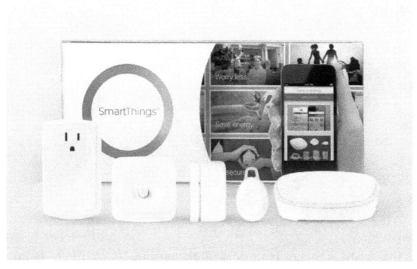

If you have seen the smart products with the SmartThings you should know that they are also compatible with the Echo device. They may be lights, power outlets, and switches. You can control any device or appliances that are plugged in with the help of the SmartThings power outlets. You can even control non-smart appliances with the Amazon Echo via SmartThings power outlets.

First, you should link the SmartThings device to the Amazon Echo through the Alexa app. To enable it, you should go to Settings and look for "Connected Home" to be able to link the smart devices from there. The Philips Hue voice commands are the same likt the voice commands that you can use.

Wink

Wink hub is a central device to help you manage Wink-compatible devices. It is similar to SmartThings, powers outlets and functions.

And this is the list of the devices that are compatible with both Wink hub and Amazon Echo:

- Commercial Electric
  - Smart LED Downlight
- Cree
  - Connected LED Bulb
- EcoSmart
  - Smart A19
  - Smart PAR20
  - Smart GU10
  - Smart BR30
- GE
  - Link A19
  - Link BR30
  - Link PAR38
- Leviton
  - Z-wave Scene Capable Dimmer
  - Z-wave Scene Capable Switch
  - Z-wave Scene Capable Receptacle
  - Z-wave Scene Capable Plug-In Module
  - Z-wave Scene Capable Plug-In Appliance Module
- Lutron
  - Caseta Plug-On Lamp Dimmer
  - Caseta In-Wall Dimmer

- Osram
    - Lightly White-tunable Smart LED Bulb
- Philips
    - Hue A19
    - Hue BR30
- TCP
    - A19 Bulb

Insteon

The Amazon Echo is also compatible with Insteon hub, except SmartThings and Wink. Sll the devices plugged in the Insteon hub may be controlled. The only compatible Insteon hub so is the Hub 2245 – 222. If you pair this hub to the Alexa app you will be able to use the Echo in triggering connected appliances and lights.

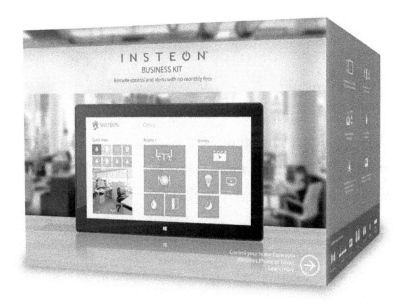

WeMo

 You can also pair WeMo devices with the Amazon Echo. Your Echo will detect the WeMo device automatically when you connect it to the same Wi-Fi network. Here is the list of the WeMo devices which are compatible with the Amazon Echo:

- WeMo Switch
- WeMo Light Switch
- WeMo Insight

It is easy to connect these devices to the Wi-Fi by using the WeMo app. The Amazon Echo is able detect them automatically. You should know that the voice commands for the Amazon Echo are the same like the Philips Hue voice commands.

Chapter 8: How to Create Smart Home Skills

Your Echo is able to make your home smart. And Smart Home Skill (SHS) will help you with it as it you can create skills that control cloud-connected devices across your Wi-Fi network. You can do so many things using this technology.

First of all, you should use the Smart Home Skill API to build a SHS. You will get less control as a developer but it will simplify the development process. Using SHS, you won't need to make the voice user interface.

The Smart Home Skill API is able to define the requests and the words that you say to make these requests. The requests that the skill can handle are known as device directives. This device directive may be turned on or turned off, and the user could say, for example, "turn on the living-room lights."

You can be a developer of this SHS and you can define how your skills may respond to a specific device directive. You should follow the same example and write the code to make the living-room light turn on and off. It is called a *skill adapter*.

You will need the following to make a SHS:

- An Amazon developer account. You should visit this website to register for free: https://developer.amazon.com/
- A cloud-enabled device that you would like to control and use through Alexa. For example, lights.
- An AWS (Amazon Web Service) account. You can host your skill as an AWS Lambda function, using this account.
- Basic knowledge of OAuth 2.0.
- Basic knowledge of Node.js, Java, or Python.

- An Alexa-enabled device for testing (Amazon Echo, Echo Dot, or Fire TV).

How to Build a Smart Home Skill

Step 1: Create a Skill

1. First, open the Amazon Developer Portal and log in. Then click *Apps and Services* and Choose *Alexa*. Click *Get Started* and Choose *Add a New Skill*. It will open a page named *Skill Information*. You should select *Smart Home Skill API* and enter the name of your skill. Then Click *Save* and copy the *Application ID* to your clipboard by right clicking and then select *Copy*. You should save this in a note on your desktop.

Step 2: Create a Lambda Function

1. First, create an AWS account if you do not have it. Then log into the AWS Management Console and select AWS Lambda. Then you should define the *Region* in the top right-hand corner by choosing from the dropdown list.
You should know that Lambda functions for Alexa must be hosted by this region.

2. Then click *Create a Lambda function* and select *alexa-smart-home-skill-adapter* from the blueprint page. You should type "Home" into the filter box to find this blueprint quickly.

3. Then you should set the *Event Source Type* to *Alexa Smart Home* and Add an *Application ID* from the developer portal. This is copied to your clipboard. And click *Next*.

4. Then enter *Name* and *Description* for your skill. You should select *Python 2.7* for the *Runtime*. You are also able to use Node.js or Java. Then check that *Edit Code Inline* is selected.

5. And then enter the following code into the code editor.

You should know that this code is only a start. This code defines the request type and the response is not fully implemented. Remember that you will need to handle every type of request that a user could make to your skill and provide all the necessary responses.

- You should remember not to change the *Handler* default name from *lambda_function.lambda_handler*. Remember that function handler is the main entry point for a Lambda function.

The file name in the console will be *lambda_function* and the *lambda_handler* function will be the entry point.

- Next, select *Lambda_basice_execution* from the *Role options*. You should leave all of the *Advanced Settings* as they are and set *to defaults*. Then click *Next*.

- And check that all the shown information is correct. Then click *Create Function*.

- Once your function has been completed a summary page will appear. You should copy the Amazon Resource Name (ARN) in the top right-hand corner. You will need this information to configure the smart home skill in the developer portal.

Step 3: Register Your Skill

1. First, open the Amazon Developer Portal and log in. Then click *Apps and Services* and Choose *Alexa*. Then select your skill from the list and click through the *Interaction Model Tab* until you reach the page named *Configuration*. You should copy the ARN number from the Lambda function into the *Endpoint* field and enable *Account Linking*. For this you will need this information:

- Authorization URL
- Client ID

- Redirect URL

- Authorization Grant Type— make sure *Authorization Code Grant is* selected.

  you will need to provide the following information for Authorization Grant Type:

  > Access Token URI: (The URL for the OAuth Server)

  > Client Secret: (It is necessary for Alexa service to be able to authenticate with the Access Token URI.)

  > Client Authentication Scheme: (It identifies the type of authentication Alexa has to use)

  > Privacy Policy URL: (You need a URL for a page with your privacy policy. This link is shown in the Alexa app and it is necessary for smart home skills.)

2. Then choose *Yes* to enable testing.

Step 4: Test Your Skill

You will need to use an Alexa-enabled device to test your skill

1. First, open the Lambda Console and select your smart home skill. Then click on *Event Source* Tab and select *Alexa Smart Home* . You should make sure *State* is enabled, then save and close Lambda Console.

2. Then open the Alexa App and click *Skills*. Then you should enter the name of your smart home skill and Search. Then *Enable* and *Account-link* your skill to the device cloud it is made to work with.

3. Then click the *Smart Home* tab on the home screen of the Alexa App and choose *Your Devices*. Then you should give Alexa commands using the utterances you have programmed your skill. It is necessary to support with the device names you've set for the devices in your account. This account is linked to the device cloud.

4. You should repeat Step 3 until you are satisfied.

Step 5: Submit Your Skill

1. First, open the developer portal and click on the *Alexa Section*. Then choose *Get Started* and select your smart home skill.

   Then you should click *Next* until you reach *Publishing*

Information.

On this stage fill in *Short Skill* and *Full Skill* descriptions.

Make sure that *Category* is set to *Smart Home.*

Then add *Keywords* if you desire.

Then you should add small and large icons so they could meet the described guidelines. Then add any testing instructions for the certification team. Then click *Next* and answer the questions about *Privacy and Compliance.* Then click *Submit for Certification.*

Step 6: Maintenance

After publishing your skill it is recommended to keep maintaining it. You should enhance features, fix bugs, and improve your experience with it.

Chapter 9: Resetting the Echo and Troubleshooting Issues

The Amazon Echo is quite unique device but, as any kind of technology, sometimes it needs resetting. If Alexa does not respond properly to your commands or your Wi-Fi is not connecting properly you should reset your Echo. Whatever streaming issues you may have with your Echo your first essential step must be restarting your device. You should just press and hold down the Microphone and Volume down buttons at the same time to make restart of your Echo.

You should do it until the light ring on your Echo turns orange. Once it's complete the light ring should turn blue. Then it illuminates blue it will turn on and off again. Your device should be ready for regular use and you should setup Wi-Fi if needed.

Another case is when the companion application may become unresponsive.

It may happen when the skills backing up the Alexa software as your mobile application is constantly being updated. If you have received a message stating that the "The Alexa app is offline", there are many solutions to fix this error. Here are the solutions you should follow:

1. **Restarting your mobile device** – It is a common way to fix small issues in application.

You can fix any unresponsiveness using this way.

2. **Force close the application** – If you force closing the application it may also aid in solving in immediate issues. You can also have the option to clear data for the Alexa companion application in some devices if desired. As Amazon recommends you should clear the data and select "Force Stop".

3. **Uninstall and reinstall the Application** – One of the ways to clear up any issues within the Alexa application is uninstalling the application. After uninstalling the application you should navigate to your respective app store and re-download the application

How to Solve Connection & Streaming Issues with the Echo Dot

Normally your Wi-Fi connection determines the connection issues with the Echo. You may have troubleshoot and rectify these issues in many ways. Here are some common fixes:

- **Restart Your Amazon Echo** can be the most common fix for any connectivity issues.
- **Reduce Wi-Fi Congestion** – You can reduce your Wi-Fi congestion by turning off devices that are not being used. It will free up some much needed bandwidth on your network.
  If you raise the device from the ground or keep it away from any walls it may help in keeping the lines of connection open. If it does not solve the issue you should move your device closer to the router/modem so it may improve the connection.

- **Restart Your Network Device** – If you have some issues with the network connectivity of your Echo you should reset the modem. It may be another way to fix when troubleshooting.
- **Contact Your Internet Service Provider** – If none of the above fixes does not help you, you should contact your Internet Service Providers. Also, if you

know that it is not an issue with your Amazon Echo device and you still have this problem, you should contact your Internet Service Provider for more help troubleshooting your network connection.

Bluetooth Connection Issues with Your Amazon Echo

One of the complications that may arise while interacting with your Echo is a Bluetooth issue. There are many things you can do to fix a Bluetooth connectivity issues and here is the list of fixes:

- **Interference** – It includes a number of various items. These are electronic devices that may block your signal. Baby monitors, microwaves and various other wireless devices may be common interference items too.

If your Bluetooth connectivity does not function properly you should move your device away from anything that may interfere with the connection.

- **Battery Life of your Mobile Device** – You should know that the battery life of your mobile device may also interfere with capability to connect by Bluetooth. You should make sure that the device has a full charge if your device has a battery that is not able to be removed. You should replace or recharge the batteries if your device has removable and (or) rechargeable batteries.

- **Delete all prior Bluetooth Devices** – If you have any connectivity issues you should clear and reconnect the Bluetooth device. It may aid in rectifying any connectivity issues. To clear your Bluetooth device, you should navigate to

Settings within the Mobile Alexa companion application, from within the left navigation panel. Then, inside of Settings, you should select the Alexa

Device that you are having issues with and select
Bluetooth > clear.

- **Add a New Bluetooth Device** – One of the
  simplest ways to test if a Bluetooth connection is
  working properly is to delete all old devices and
  reconnect a new one. You can do it by selecting your
  Alexa device, selecting Bluetooth> Pair a New Device.
  When your device enters pairing mode you should
  select the device from your cellular device. And then
  Alexa will confirm if your device has been connected
  successfully.

Chapter 10: How You Can Use Your Echo

The Amazon Echo is able to perform lots of things. It can helpful in any specific area of the home.

Using Your Echo in the Kitchen

The Echo can be helpful not only in the bedroom, living room, bathroom but also in the kitchen. It is able to perform lots of tasks to help you with working in the kitchen.

1. Maintaining your grocery list

Making any list may become easy with Alexa. You can make any kind of lists and shopping lists are the ones that are the most compatible with the Echo. You should tell Alexa the item and the list which you would like to add the corresponding item and it will be done at once. For example, you can say "Alexa, please add flour to my Grocery List"

You can edit and update all your lists without speaking directly to Alexa within the Alexa app. You should just select Shopping & To Do lists.

2. How to Use Alexa to Convert Kitchen Units

One of the most helpful skills while cooking is that Alexa is able to convert units to match an altered serving size of a recipe. Sometimes it is hard to do when your hands are busy. And Alexa can help you with it.

You should know that Alexa is able to answer general metric and simple questions. You can simply say, "Alexa convert 5 cups to pints" and she will do it for you.

3. How to Use Alexa to Make Your Morning Coffee

You can do so many things with all of the smart home integrations and even make your morning coffee. You just need to achieve a simple drip coffee maker and a smart switch. To enable this skill, you should go into IFTTT and create a recipe to run on the smart switch plug. To provide a proper work, you must add your coffee grounds and water to your coffee pot the night before. This is one thing that Echo cannot do for you. Once it is done when you wake up and you should say your trigger phrase and the coffee should be ready when you are.

4. How to Use Alexa to Start Timers

Timers are very helpful in the kitchen. You can use
them to determine quickly when food is done or when
your cake must come out of the oven. You should
simply say "Alexa, start a new time for 15 minutes
from now". When 15 minutes have passed you will
hear the Echo's speaker until you stop it.

You can also set multiple timers at once with Alexa. It
does not matter what is the length of time, you can
check the status of your timers by simply asking
Alexa. You can also cancel timers if it is needed.

5. Use the Echo to Control appliances

IFTTT included lots of integrated appliances. You are
able to control all the devices integrated with your Echo.
For example, you can control your dishwasher, oven or
even your slow cooker with Alexa enabled device.

But first you will need to create applets within the
appropriate appliance service in IFTTT to enable these
devices. These applets usually use Amazon Alexa as the
trigger.

6. Use Alexa to generate Recipe ideas

One of the things that can be handled through the Alexa skills is finding recipes. There are lots of skills that you can use while searching for unique recipes using your Echo.

Here are some skills:

Recipe Finder by Ingredient:

You can find recipes based on the items that they currently have in their possession, using this skill. You can ask about the type of dish that you want to make and get ideas from this application. You should say some alike commands to enable this skill:

"Alexa, ask Recipe Finder by Ingredient what kind of sandwich can I make with Swiss cheese"
"Alexa, ask Recipe Finder by Ingredient what I can make with potatoes and mushrooms"

Trending Recipes & Food:

You can get the top recipes on Reddit Food within the last 24 hours with this skill. You will get the requested recipes via a link in a card in the Alexa application. You should remember that this content must be user submitted. You can say some alike commands to enable this skill:
"Alexa, can I have the fifth recipe from Trending Recipes"
"Alexa, get the latest recipe from Trending Recipes"
"Alexa, give me the most recent recipe in Trending Recipes" recipe

Best Recipes:

You can enable this skill free. Using this skill, you can tell Alexa what ingredients you have to work with and it will provide you with three ingredients that suit your needs. You can narrow down the recipe choice by time of day or dish type. It concerns the options of breakfast, lunch or dinner. You can browse recipes and choose the one which is most attractive to you. You should say some commands like these ones to enable this skill:

"Alexa, please open Best Recipes"
"Alexa, ask best recipes what's for lunch"
"Alexa, ask best recipes what's for dinner"

These are not all the recipe skills that you can use with the Echo. You can find other applications in the skills library that are able to give you interesting cooking ideas.

7. How to Use Alexa to Count & Maintain Calories

If you keep a diet or you like healthy lifestyle Alexa is able to help you with counting calories without enabling a skill. She is able to tell you how many calories certain foods have. You should remember that Alexa does not know about all foods but she knows the basics.
Alexa also knows nutritional information like carbohydrates. If it is a wide spread information she will tell you all about food. If you ask about generic foods you can get back lots of information.

8. How to Use Alexa to find wine Pairing Information

Wine Buddy is a skill to give the best pairing options with certain dishes. You should simply enable Wine Buddy in the Alexa application.
It is easy to use this skill by asking your Echo "Alexa, what can I serve with fried salmon?" And it will give you recommendations what would match with your chosen dish.

This skill is getting more and more advanced so you should keep the requests basic to get the accurate answers.

9. Use Alexa for Drink recipes & Ideas

If you are planning some holiday party and you need some beverage ideas Alexa is able to help you with that. She will suggest a number of cool refreshing cocktail to match your mood and company. Here are the skills that you can use: Easy Cocktail, Suggest Me a Cocktail and Mixologist. The beverages in this category are not suitable for all ages so the users should be age 21 and up.

Easy Cocktail: This skill provides recipes for various cocktails.

You can enable this skill by saying such commands:

"Alexa, ask easy cocktail how to make a classic margarita"

"Alexa, ask Easy Cocktail how you make a fuzzy navel"

Using Your Echo to Tell Bedtime Stories

If you have no time to tell bedtime story to your children the Echo can do it for you as it is able to keep children entertained with the Short Bedtime Story skill. The duration of each of the stories within this skill is about 30 seconds to one-minute long. They may also include the name of your choice to be more personalized.

You can find several different stories in the application of different plots and story twists. There are even stories related to popular Minions. You can choose the stories that take place in a galaxy or Alexa is able to tell you a story about a kid getting elected as president. Some stories may not be suitable for bedtime but other ones are good enough to lull your child.

Information on the Latest Features

It is always easy to understand what updates have been made to Alexa. Sometimes you might need to read a newsletter or subscribe to some email listing but it is not compulsory. You should just say "Alexa, what new features do you have?" You should also know when something is added or pushed to the Echo Dot, Alexa will explain you what it is. You should simply ask for an explanation and you will get it.

Workouts

The Workout may also become quick and easy process with your Amazon Echo. You will not have any excuses why you can't do small workout in during the day after enabling the 7 Minute Workout skill. If you don't have time or you don't like gyms it is a great alternative to use 7 Minute Workout.

You can enable the "7-Minute Workout" skill within the Amazon Alexa companion mobile application and you will get a quick workout that takes 7 minutes to complete. This workout is perfect for getting energized before your working day starts or you can get in some quick activity before bed.

Once you have enabled it in the Alexa app, you can start your workout by saying "Alexa, start 7-minute workout". These workouts include so many kinds of exercises like jumping jacks, pushups, wall sits, squats, and much more.

You can also see the images inside the Alexa application just to make sure that you are doing all of the moves correctly.

Always Add More Skills to Learn More

Originally the Echo already has a number of skills enabled. Some of the them are basic and the other skills may be enabled within the Alexa app to take your Echo on another level.

You can enable thousands of skills online, from the Alexa app or even from talking directly to Alexa. You can update new skills every day.

If you want to get a complete listing of skills you should simply open the Alexa app, choose the menu button and select the word Skills. You can browse the skills by category and enable the items you like most of all.

If you want to learn more cooking and various recipes, you should simply enable the Mom's Cooking skill. Using this skill, you can get recipes for everything. You should just say: "Alexa, ask Mom's cooking for a cookie recipe".

You can control everything that the Echo is able to perform. Alexa has got a great diversity of categories and activities. Anybody can find something according to his taste and interest. It is also important to remember the commands or the names of the applications associated with them to enable certain skills.

Ask My Buddy

Ask My Buddy is a useful emergency alert system that you can use when you need some help. This application may be configured to call a friend, family member or caretaker. You can also send a text message, email or make an actual phone call with this application.

This application proves that Alexa can be also a concerned assistant. Especially this skill is good for children, individuals who are sick or senior citizens. This skill is connected directly to the functionality of the mobile device.

This skill shows that Alexa is able to become more than virtual assistant device. The software has been incorporated into wheelchairs and it might be soon an abundance of other medical devices.

The Ask My Buddy skill was included in Alexa Customers Top Pick list for 2016.

Fitbit

Fitbit was one of the most downloaded applications last Christmas in 2015. This skill provides information about your activity, sleep patterns and various other information related to your health. And it also provides measurements like your resting heart rate.

You should know that the Integration with Alexa and the Echo cannot sync or even log water and food consumption for this moment. It will be changed in the near future to make logging food and drink easier.

Find your phone

If you have lost your cellular device and there is nobody around to call you. Don't worry. Alexa is able to help you with it too.

Alexa has got many various options to accomplish this. There are some skills that require the installation of a companion application on the cellular device and some others have the ability to ring the device on command. Once you have enabled the skill by configuring the setting with the Alexa applicant, you should simply say "Alexa, find my phone" and your device will ring loudly even if it was on silent.

IFTTT recipes may be also helpful if you set them. But you should make sure that triggers are in place if you lose your device and the key phrase must be spoken.

Chapter 11: Google Home Vs. Amazon Echo

These two devices the Amazon Echo and the Google Home have their own features but the winner is obvious. The success of the Amazon Echo has predetermined the appearance of the similar products in the market of smart devices.

The Google Home was released in October of 2016. It is designed to perform similarly to the Google Assistant on a smart phone.

However, the Amazon Echo products and the Google Home differ in many ways. The first difference is the price of the device. The original Amazon Echo cost $179.99 while the Google Home cost $129. Both devices require either an Android or IOS operating system. The Google Home has specific version requirements. And the Amazon Echo is compatible with Fire OS and it is accessible via your computer's web browser.

But there are some distinctions between the Google Home and the Amazon Echo.

Google Home may be described as "a voice-activated speaker powered by the Google Assistant." And it can be the greatest Amazon Echo's competitor. The Google Home is able also to control household items like temperature or lights. Google has managed to create a great device.

The Google Home may become a helpful option if you use Google Calendar, Google Maps or any Google run applications. The users will like the device which is integrated with technology they are already utilizing.

The Amazon Echo is designed more like a smart home hub and it is able to play music via different streaming services.

You can control this device with your voice and it gives you a lot of possibilities and functionalities.

The Amazon Echo and the Google Home both have a great look. But you should better place them on a shelving unit.

The Amazon Echo has a shape of a small tower. It has seven microphones that is why it easily picks up the sound from any direction. The Google Home has a form of a small vase that looks like more an air freshener with a swappable base. You can swap the base for a variety of colors that suits your environment best of all.

Conversations with Amazon Echo and Google Home

One of the greatest advantages of the Google Home is its skill of conversation that the Amazon Echo should yet adopt. When you start your conversation with the Google Home it is able to understand your sentences and keep up the conversation.

You cannot make the same conversation with the Amazon Echo. To continue your talk with Alexa you should say each time the word "Alexa".

The Amazon Echo is able to answer the basic questions but Alexa is not for conversations. Alexa is mostly a robot for answering questions and performing tasks.

Making Shopping with Alexa and Google Home

The Amazon Echo enables you to make shopping via your voice and the Google Home has no such integration for making purchases. So the Google Home is not able to make purchases.

Playing Music

One of the differences of the Amazon Echo and the Google Home have is the music capabilities. Unlike the Amazon Echo, the Google home is able to integrate well with YouTube. The Amazon Echo has no such option. If you have not set the music subscription services within the Alexa settings properly, the Echo will not be able to comprehend your request.

The Amazon Echo and the Google Home also have differences in understanding commands. If you ask the Echo to play some soundtrack from the movie it will play the real soundtrack of some movie. But if you give the same command to Google Home it will play the specific song that associates this movie.

As for the other music services, the Amazon Echo may not perform with YouTube unlike good operation with Spotify. When you say "Play Spotify", the Echo will start playing the application that is topped listening in your list. But the Google Home will play in a random location.

Among other integrations except YouTube and Spotify, the Google Home also works with Google Play Music, Pandora and TuneIn. The Echo and different Amazon Alexa enabled products work Spotify, Pandora, Amazon Music, TuneIn and others.

Interacting with Your Home

The Amazon Echo is undisputable winner in competing with the Google Home for interactions within the Home. The Echo can connect a great variety of Brands for creating a smart home such as Nest, Honeywell, SmartThings, Wink, Insteon, Belkin WeMo, Ecobee, Lifx, Big Ass Fans,Philips Hue, IFTTT, Control4, Crestron, and other devices that may be programmed with Alexa Skills and IFTTT.

The Google Home is able to connect currently with Nest, Belkin WeMo, Honeywell, SmartThings, Philips Hue, IFTTT. When utilizing the Amazon Echo and the Google Home as a smart home controller you can see the difference by saying "Turn on the lights". If you say this command to the Echo it will interpret it to turn on the light in a specific room whereas the Google Home will turn on all of the lights in the house or apartment. For someone it doesn't make much difference but for someone it does. You should make specifications on a room-by-room basis.

The user's commands for the Echo may be more flexible and they may combine different light combinations. The command "Turn on the lights" may trigger the hall lights, a light in the bedroom and the living room instead of one room.

What is Better?

Before purchasing the Google Home, you should know that it is able to support only one main user account. This is the account that is used with the calendar when you set up the Google Home. This device is suitable for the users that do not have multiple accounts. And it is not suitable for the people who have multiple calendars. It is better if one person uses this device.

Unlike the Google Home, the Echo can utilize various household profiles. This way the multiple users are able to modify the features like the shopping list. These features are shared within Alexa. And the authorized adults are also able to use any payment information on the Amazon Echo.

If you are looking for a proper size, versatility and intelligence on choosing between the Amazon Echo and the Google Home then the Amazon Echo is definitely for you.

The Echo is able to do so much that there is no wonder that many people love it a lot. Besides, the Echo is the only one in a line of many devices which is able to speak to Alexa. She is able not only to control home devices but also to keep necessary information at your fingertips. The Echo provides the versatility you need and it is a perfect home control device.

Alexa is able to do so many things and tell about so much helpful information. She can tell the weather forecast, describe the state of traffic on your commute to work and order pizza if you are ungry. Just ask Alexa and she is ready to help you.

Alexa is able to become more than a virtual assistant. She is able to learn and it is being updated all the time. This is one of the reasons why the Amazon Alexa enabled devices are dominating the home hub market. You will be always organized, prepared, on time and entertained with Alexa.

Overall

Both the Amazon Echo and the Google Home are good devices. The Echo is more suitable for everyday listening. You can use it for playing radio stations, music from the services like Spotify and Pandora, and music from your library. The Echo is also able to play Google Play, downloads or any music from Apple Music once it is setup through a Bluetooth connection. You can also pair your Echo with the Amazon Tap or Amazon Echo.

The Google Home is a better conversationalist as it is able to understand the context of various questions from the users. It is also able to retrieve data from the Internet and to play music but with poorer quality. You can also play games like Mad Libs or basic trivia games with the Google Home. It is even able to control speakers in different rooms through Google home application or by voice commands. If you are a Google user then the Google Home may be a good companion for you.

Choosing among these two devices, the Amazon Echo and the Google Home, the choice may depend on your lifestyle and what is important for you.

Conclusion

The Amazon Echo is able to perform a great variety of skills and tasks. It can stream music and Podcasts from different sources including Amazon Prime, Spotify, IHEartRadio, TuneIn or Pandora.

The Amazon Echo can be awakened by speaking one of the wake words like Alexa, Amazon or Echo.

This smart gadget is able to look up facts, tell jokes and give general information. You can set alarms and timers for your activities, make to-do lists, read books, control your home and many other things.

Beside all this features, the Echo may be used as a hub for all your smart home tasks. The list of appliances that work with the Echo is growing. Here are some of the most common utilities:

- Nexia smart home
- Crestron smart home
- Lutron Lighting sets
- Haiku smart lights
- Belkin Switches
- SmartThings home platform
- Wink home platform
- Insteon home platform
- August Lock
- Scout Security system
- Ecobee3 Thermostat
- Philips Hue Bulb
- LIFX Bulbs
- Ledvance Bulbs
- Nest Thermostat
- Logitech Harmony Hub entertainment controller
- Control4 smart home

The new items that will work with the Amazon Echo and Alexa are being added every day. There are over 3000 skills which enable Alexa to do lots of tasks.

The Amazon Echo is also able to recognize your voice and it can also give you the option of adding various audio features.

Despite the new competition emerging everyday Amazon's

devices such as the Amazon Echo, Amazon Tap and the Amazon Echo Dot stay in the lead for smart home/virtual assistant devices.

Among big variety of alternatives to suite of Alexa-based products none is able to match the functionality and compatibility of the Amazon Alexa products.

Thank you for reading. I hope you enjoy it. I ask you to leave your honest feedback.

I think next books will also be interesting for you:

Amazon Echo

Amazon Echo Dot

AMAZON ECHO DOT

The Ultimate User Guide to
Amazon Echo Dot
2nd Generation for Beginners

Andrew Howard

Amazon Echo Dot

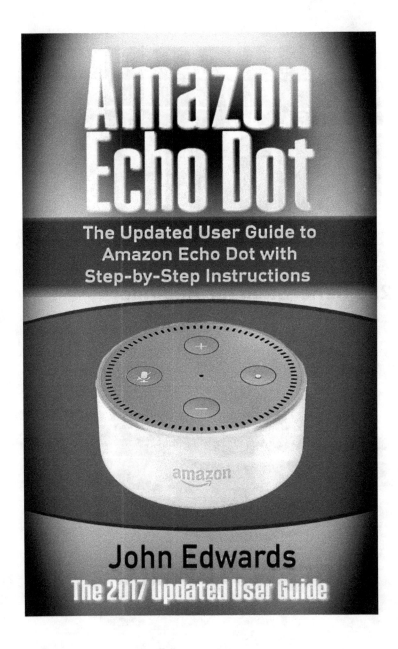

www.ingramcontent.com/pod-product-compliance
Lightning Source LLC
Chambersburg PA
CBHW071224050326
40689CB00011B/2450